From the Attic

SELECTED VERSE
1965-2015

From the Attic

SELECTED VERSE
1965-2015

ANTHONY HARRINGTON

Kudzu Editions
Alpharetta, Georgia

Kudzu Editions
P.O. Box 5005
Alpharetta, GA 30023

ISBN 978-0-9963492-1-5
Library of Congress Control Number: 2015957672

Cover Image: "Der arme Poet" ("The Poor Poet"), 1839 painting by Carl Spitzweg. Neue Pinakothek, Munich, Germany

10 9 8 7 6 5 4 3 2   1 2 0 9 1 5

Printed by BookLogix
Alpharetta, Georgia

∞This paper meets the requirements of ANSI/NISO Z39.48-1992 (Permanence of Paper)

Again and always,
to Natalie, who loves *Acid Time*

ACKNOWLEDGMENTS

Some of these verses appeared in the following publications: *Atlanta Review, The Chattahoochee Review, The Classical Outlook, The Christian Century, Daimon, Drastic Measures, The Epigrammatist, Four Quarters, Light Quarterly, The Lilliput Review, The Lyric, The Midwest Poetry Review, Poultry, The Saturday Review, The Tinhorn Press, TRINACRIA, The Wallace Stevens Journal*, and *Western Humanities Review*. Thanks to the editors for their kind acceptances.

Some of the verses in this book were originally published in the poetry volumes *Tersery Versery* (Hendricks Publishing, 1982) and *The Man in the Goodwill Bin* (The Tinhorn Press, 1987).

Other verses in this collection were published in the following limited-edition chapbooks:

Acid Time (Kudzu Books, 1977)
The Ballads of Eskimo Nell & Others (The Tinhorn Press, 1987)
By Poets Provoked (Kudzu Pamphlets, 1992)
Scrimshaw: Quatrains and Clerihews (Kudzu Pamphlets, 1993)
Nominal Verse: Clerihews (Kudzu Pamphlets, 1998)
The Jerusalem Rooster (Kudzu Pamphlets, 2001)
The Old Formalist (Kudzu Pamphlets, 2003)
Subscriptions: Epigraphical Verse (Kudzu Pamphlets, 2005)
Quatrains (Kudzu Pamphlets, 2010)
Quadrivia (Kudzu Pamphlets, 2012)
Harrington's Couplets (Kudzu Pamphlets, 2013)
Ms. Muse & Me (Kudzu Pamphlets, 2013)
Sundries (Kudzu Pamphlets, 2014)

CONTENTS

* All of the double dactyls begin with the first line "Higgledy-piggledy." They are listed in this table of contents by their second line.

from *The Man in the Goodwill Bin* (1987)

from *By Poets Provoked* (1992)

from *Scrimshaw: Quatrains & Clerihews* (1993)

QUATRAINS

from *The Ballads of Eskimo Nell & Others* (1995)

from *Nominal Verse: Clerihews* (1998)

from *The Jerusalem Rooster* (2001)

from *The Old Formalist* (2003)

from *Subscriptions: Epigraphical Verse* (2005)

from *Quatrains* (2010)

from *Quadrivia* (2012)

from *Harrington's Couplets* (2013)

from *Ms. Muse & Me* (2013)

from *Sundries* (2014)

Uncollected Verse

AUTHOR'S NOTE

This book is a selection of verse written over a period of fifty or more years. I use the word verse, not poetry, deliberately since only occasionally does something I wrote gain lift enough to be judged a poem. Let the reader decide which ones (if any) in the following pages deserve the name poem.

I chose *From the Attic* as the title because it aptly describes the jumble inside this book's covers. I was raised in an old tall house that luckily had an attic in which I spent many happy hours rummaging around in the things stored there—boxes of out-of-fashion clothes, books, old newspapers, broken furniture, photo albums, old Christmas ornaments, and so on. It was a place of dusty and dimly-lit discovery.

A casual flipping of the book's pages will reveal a great variety of forms: quatrains, couplets, clerihews, double dactyls, dramatic monologues, a sonnet or two, triolets, ballads, epigrams, and even some free verse. A closer reading will show samples of both serious and humorous items. The only unity this book has is the simple, single mind of its author, happy to have hauled down from the attic of memory and observation such a mingling of many forms.

Versifiers and poets are ones who make things out of words. W.H. Auden called such things "verbal contraptions." He suggested that when we are presented with such a verbal contraption we ask two questions: how does it work and what does it tell me about the person who made it.

My verbal contraptions are very simple; how they work is pretty clear. My hope for the second question is that they show that the person who made them tried hard to instruct and delight, and deserves forgiveness for his lapses and errors.

Johns Creek, Georgia
August 2015

from *Acid Time* (1977)

My Learnèd Friends

They told me that I should not rhyme,
That scanning is a sin.
Can I help it if, from time to time,
My bones demand a skin?

Be loose, they said, but loose with grace
And let your lines run free,
Ignoring that two shores embrace
Even the wildest sea.

Following meter's mad intent
They said would lead to Hell.
I know the thought they really meant:
My poems will never sell.

They may be right, my learnèd friends.
They get the grants, not I,
But like a diver risking bends
I surge to form's blue sky.

So on I'll write with thumb to nose
Poems that chime like clocks.
In a world that pools with prose,
I choose to throw some rocks.

Acid Time

I wore beauty's beauty once.
I wore it, yes, and grace.
The people looked to me for truth.
I saw it in each face.

I've scarred myself with acid time.
The people look away.
I groan. Disfigured, now I have
Some truthful things to say.

Between Engagements

When the faded ghosts of vaudeville stars
Go back to their glory scenes
They pass right through revivalists
Or porno movie screens.

Where once their voices soared in tune
Or their feet both bucked and wung
X-Rated flickers barely play
Or Gospel songs get sung.

In broken letters on broad marquees
Where their names shone forth in lights
Their troubled spirit eyes can read
Jesus Saves   Steamy Nights.

I know something of the troubled hell
Where souls like theirs now burn.
I've toured some places in my past
To which I can't return.

Overexposure

I throw the shutter of my sight
And pinhole being in its light.
In the album called This Is
I would mount clear images.

But in the darkroom of my mind
When the rolls of film unwind
My thought's camera only give
Blurred and faded negatives.

Lines for the Single-Minded

Harbor firemen called one day
To save a burning ship
Poured so much water's weight on her
She sank beside her slip.

Coiling their hoses, they looked smug,
Their work over and complete.
Never had they known before
A fire nipped so neat.

Their task was putting out the blaze.
Oh, smiling was each face.
Where flames had leaped there leaked up steam.
Bleak bubbles proved their case.

These bell the moral home once more:
Who wins the battle can lose the war.

To an Academic

You scrape down being's dirty bones
And mount them stiff on stands.
Then velvet-rope them round to keep
Away the public's hands.

All bones and air-between you heap
Your white museum frames,
And on the charts of all that chalk
You list long Latin names.

About your work I softly walk
And just as soft retreat,
For I am certain of a single thought:
Bones were meant for meat.

To a Worried Friend

You ask in letters for some lines
Of my life, my work, my growth:
I study daily Georgia pines
And imitate their sloth.
I root myself a personal zone
And strive to fill the space around
By dropping now and then a cone
Or at least a needle to the ground.
And do I meet with much success?
I put such questions to my trees
Who are, as I am, more or less
In litter almost to the knees.
Some things are sprouting in the dark
That will in the light bear up my bark.

Driving North

On a Florida road
Less black than grey
The sun made checks
Through all the day
With the wide *V* shadows
Of birds of prey
Who matched my thoughts
Along the way.

New England Song

I noted the way a birch or two
Can sometimes bring whole woods in view.

Of how in winter the birches say
Not everything in the world goes grey.

Of how in summer their bark is seen
Making waves in all that green.

Then I remembered sly Robert Frost
Writing as a boy on birches tossed.

A better poet with better lines.
I'd better write my poem on pines.

Song in August

Crickets tonight in the woods nearby
Choir out their pain, their joy.
My fortieth summer sounds the same
As when I was a boy.

Have identical crickets followed me
Through space and down the years?
Perhaps, for on this head I bend
I bear the same old ears.

Insects that Homer listened to
Are chanting just outside.
I think that they'll be singing so
When all of us have died.

Not many summers more will I
Be audient to such verse.
"Sing, crickets," I whisper half aloud,
"As I, your prayers, your curse."

Gallic Thrift

Better Living Through Chemistry
                    advertising slogan

Visit the ancient mills that line
The banks of Delaware's Brandywine.

Museum now, the mills still stand,
Monuments of the wisely planned.

Gunpowder makers, come from France,
Were well aware they lived by chance.

Knowing with what they worked within
They built each mill with one wall thin.

When the blast came as they knew it would,
Survivors saw that three walls stood.

Explosive mind, is that your gift?
Learn from the DuPont's Gallic thrift.

Prospects

When I am old and bent and have no teeth
Propped in a corner chair
Shameless I'll lean on my cane to leer
At the young girls passing there.

They'll laugh and say at the way I look
With my jaw hanging slack,
"Oh, keep your eye on that wicked man—
Don't dare to turn your back."

They'll reach to ruffle my thinning hair
And chuck me under my chin.
I'll know the single joy of age:
Vague memories of sin.

I long for that wonderful day to come,
The indulgence that I'll find.
Have you never noticed how only
To *old* men girls are kind?

Double Dactyls from *Tersery Versery* (1982)

Higgledy-piggledy
Painter J. Audubon
Suffered for decades
By poverty pressed

Selling the plates of his
Ornithological
Printings allowed him to
Feather his nest.

Higgledy-piggledy
Peter Bogdanovich
Makes many movies to
Which millions go.

Still, as a mortal this
Cinematographist
Someday will edit his
Last picture show.

Higgledy-piggledy
Coleridge's Mariner
Stopped him a wedding guest,
Told a long tale

Boring the man with his
Albatrossistical
Stories of when he was
Under slack sail.

Higgledy-piggledy
Congressman Dickinson
Had a young daughter his
Neighbors thought odd.

Up in her attic this
Anti-Amherstian
Scribbled short letters she
Posted to God.

Higgledy-piggledy
Thomas A. Edison
Dreamed up the phono as
Well as the light.

Thanks to this genius e-
Lectromechanical
We can read labels of
Records at night.

Higgledy-piggledy
Euclid Geometer
Pained by the asking of
"What is the use

Studying doctrines so
Axiomatical?"
Answered acutely, "Oh,
Don't be obtuse!"

Higgledy-piggledy
Faulkner the Nobelist
Serves as a model for
Novelist: South.

Faced with the prose of the
Yoknapatawphacist
Many a writer has
Shut his own mouth.

Higgledy-piggledy
Ernest M. Hemingway
Writing of matters of
Which he was full

Published some volumes
Tauromachistical,
Page after page simply
Throwing the bull.

Higgledy-piggledy
Juliette Gordon Low
Said to some gathered girls,
"Let's form a cell,

"Females can do all of those
Baden-Powellistical
Boy Scouty things and bake
Cookies as well."

Higgledy-piggledy
Stanley Frank Musial
Of all base hitters was
Never a slouch.

Students of history
Cardinological
Still speak with relish of
Stan and his crouch.

Higgledy-piggledy
Poe's Wife Virginia
Said to her husband, "Oh,
Lighten up, Ed.

"People are sick of your
Thanatographical
Writings where everyone's either
Dying or dead."

Higgledy-piggledy
Popeye the Sailorman
Cruised through the comics with
Olive so cute.

Strictly adhering to
Spinachophagia
Gave him the strength to whip
Bluto the brute.

Higgledy-piggledy
Playwriting Sophocles
Dashed off a drama called
Oedipus Rex.

All of his audience
Attic-theatrical
Cheered his depictions of
Murder and sex.

Higgledy-piggledy
Robert L. Stevenson
Scribbled the story of
Jekyll and Hyde

Showing us all what we're
Schizophreniacally
Keeping well-hidden and
Locked up inside.

Higgledy-piggledy
Calvin Stowe's Harriet
Titled her first draft as
Uncle Tom's Hut.

Got back a letter re-
Jectionslipiacal,
"I liked your novel , dear
Harriet, BUT...."

Higgledy-piggledy
Harriet Novelist
Lifted her chin and then
Cabled right back

"Bow to your wisdom so
Editoristical.
How 'bout we try it as
Uncle Tom's Shack?

Higgledy-piggledy
Harriet's Editor
Swallowed his anger and
Made this reply,

"Let's end this bickering
Titularistical.
Uncle Tom's Cabin's the
One that we'll buy."

Higgledy-piggledy
Miss Annie Sullivan
Went to Tuscumbia,
Schoolteacher meek.

Given a charge who was
Multiply-handicapped
Worked her a miracle:
Helen could speak!

Higgledy-piggledy
Booker T. Washington
Preached to the brothers, "Have
Patience and poise."

Calm in his world of the
Gradualistical
Made him an enemy:
William Du Bois.

Higgledy-piggledy
Iron Duke Wellington
Fought his way up to the
Rank of a peer

Simply by kicking a
Bonaparticular
Army at Waterloo
Right in the rear.

from *The Man in the Goodwill Bin* (1987)

The Man in the Goodwill Bin

Let fall on me your throwaways
Here on the oil-spot asphalt
Of this old shopping center.
Let fall on me the clothes you have outgrown,
The visibly-threaded,
Or the garments you have allowed the world
To convince you you have outgrown.

Widows, in your snakeskin black dresses,
Drop down on me your dead men's shoes.
I kiss each tongue.
You are not, in your sleeping alone, alone.

And you, you mothers bereft,
Cleaning your attics of the toys
Your no-longer-children children
Have left behind in passage,
To my secret place bring them, bring them.
I promise I shall handle them,
Little child like, no matter how bent, broken.
There is a child here for you forever.

Burned electric people, open your fused hands
And let tumble the bared wire appliances.
A current will leap again from pole to pole,
Despite all shocks and sparks.
Lower your television sets with no horizontal hold.
Here is one who seeks the bobbing
Snowy reruns they show forth forever.
They will stand still and shine for me.

Nor you, you bookish ones,
Do not think I am not ready to suffer
Like a collapse of cinderblocks
Your volume upon volume of Reader's Digest
Condensed Books. Though there is no light
For reading here, let them slide.
I will shake each one
And feel old bookmark letters fall.

You, my fellow citizens of this quick world,
Cover me with all that you find left over
In your hurtling, headlong lives.
For you I have chosen, monk-wise,
The deep action of receptivity.
Let the ruins descend.

Here, in the close warm darkness
Of this small and temporary place,
I shall be held down, arms out,
By all that was your formerly loved,
The remnants of what you wore,
Of what you were before.

There shall be, I say, a remaking beyond me
By men more broken even than I.
This I swear to you by the tongues
Of dead men's shoes, crossed wires, and all the rest.
There shall be a redemption.
All things shall be new and fresh and again firsthand.
This I swear in what I know is the salvageable dark.
Let fall on me your throwaways.

Crossing Chester Ferry

Late in the night the first thud of the Diesel pulses
And beneath my feet the black water to white convulses.

Deckhands wedge with chocks the last and leading cars,
Stilling them under the still wheeling stars.

Iron shudders. The Chester Ferry slips its slip,
Starting the steering of its string straight trip.

Over and over the same old here-to-there
On the ever and never the same Delaware.

The ferry is gone, like much in my youth.
There is no lasting lasts as the lasting truth.

Bound elsewhere man, slowed by the river's moat,
Has murdered with a bridge the double-bowed boat.

All that I ferry on my mind's oiled tension
Slides under the threat of a like suspension.

Memory's craft slants against the tides time takes:
Far lights, dark waters, and vanishing, vanished wakes.

State Hospital Attendant: 4 to 12 Shift

I am the orderly with keys upon my belt
Arranged according to their differing lengths.
Through every door locked against me in this maze
Of linoleum halls, I am able to pass.

When the sun slides behind the far civilian hills
Like a plastic bowl from the meal just cleared,
I rest my face against the stiff detaining screen
To stare from this high place down on the misting world.
My cheek grows briefly scarred with faint crosshatched marks
The others will be shadowed by at the sun's red and final plunge.

Night slips into the ward. Caged bulbs liven overhead.
Soon even the most active tire and fall quiet.
The last page of a worn magazine softly turns.
Talk over the last medication slurs and stops.

Blanketed forms heap upon the bolted down beds.
The innocent breath of dreams fills the darkened ward.
An old nurse with her clipboard and pencil flash
Walks her smiling and responsible census rounds.

I stand under a light that says in red Latin, "It goes out."
Awaiting my time's end, I touch through the long night hours
The puzzling confidence that lies in my cold, hard keys.

Spring Thunderstorms

The verse of the rain on the roof I'm under
Is rhymed by the sonority of classical thunder.

Blue taunts of lightning that by black windows fly
Mock the constancy of the lamp whose light I'm writing by.

The rain in stanzas repeats, "Remember when....,"
Calling to the liquid of *now* the dry bone of *then*.

All rain in April's rising is a *Memento Mori*.
Review the guttering away of your own life's story.

World outside, inside heart, both at one tonight:
Past rumblings, soft lines, a certain, uncertain light.

TV Documentary: R. F. K.

Ill at the portholed sternward look,
I watched in the grey ocean images
The aged mother speaking of her third son dead;
Followed shots of him with her grandchildren
At play on a cape in a costly sweater
To the time when he waved away on another shore.
Oh, I wove together at one the touch
Of his hair and the garment that hung
So close and thick and softly rich.

On the Aran Islands off the Irish coast,
In towns cresting white on the mounded green,
Mothers still knit in a coded stitch
The cords their fishing sons would be netted in
That, drowned, their bellied, fishbailed bodies,
Bones softened and cabled white to wool,
Might be known, then belled, and buried
Under a washed stone to knell their names.
Keen for the mothers, their knotted sons.

Neighbors

I built my house on sandy land.
See how rhythmically it sways,
But that place you placed upon the rock,
See how staidly staid it stays.

I sing in my vibratory house
In tune with each creak and shake,
Prepared to accept the crashing noise
That falling in I'll make.

You in your rocky, silent house
Sneer down on my shack below.
Yours, too, will come collapse someday,
But, oh, so dull and slow.

Candles

On a July's close Friday, the fourth,
I came to a family clustered alone
On webbed chairs in a leafy backyard
Hedging the browned high school field
In a small New Jersey township
Where the harmless fire overhead
For one day's freedom filled the night,
Where uncles drank cold-laced cans of beer
And volunteer firemen with black knit ties
Over their white shirts kept a visored watch.
There is a permanence we seek.

While stiff brushes of color scrubbed the sky
And parents kept high a running talk
To keep little children from crying
As the fierce bubbles of noise burst
Against their small delicate fisted faces,
A friend's wife with her daughters near
In the dark, dark from the full day's sun,
Growing quick and more like her each day,
A friend's wife leans near to tell me
Of a friend's daughter's death at four.
There is a permanence we seek.

27

A child more hurt from birth than we,
Dead at four against the ruled white walls
Of the thick-papered institution,
Impossible to be other than heartless,
Her fevered breath unable to lift
One gasp more upon the last,
Like Thérèse's child at the foot of the flight.
Lightly like the burned black letters
Where light had been written slanting,
She falls to the form of the raised grey pages.
There is a permanence we seek.

So was my brother's life, his death.
A brief ascent, a sudden rose, then ruin.
Yet he lines under my eyelids closed
By the telling of a friend's daughter's death
And will be seen so when others lean
To tell later in the dark of later deaths.
Like the casings that carry phosphorous down
In this different, now darkened neighborhood,
Ready to sear the flesh and bubble skin,
Short lives and deaths threaten us with life.
There is a permanence we seek.

Over all this land never far from war,
Sending young men into the wet rice fields
Under such flares, mortared, such noise,
In terror, driven insane, unsafe,
Keep growing these huge night flowers,
Now monstrous blooms for all young deaths,
At four, nineteen, at any age, bright growths.
The thick summer air carries cut flowers,
Sucking life inward from the edges,
Now with the look of the all-night watch.
There is a permanence we seek.

Above our bent back heads went stalking up
The thin, faint line and then the leaves
And bursts—tulip, rose, and goldenrod,
Tiger lily—out and down and out again,
Wheeling and arching, spray after spray.
Even in museums, softly, while we sleep,
They fade on us, flowers, unaware.
Cézanne's and van Gogh's sunfilled oils
Slide, too, under the glass, the glaze,

Their age-long sure, slow droop to death.
There is a permanence we seek.

At the end of the night, my friend's wife
Gathered her girls in a rush of arms
And looked to me over their blonde heads
As over encore flowers presented to a diva.
Planted in her arms, they waved away
To reach after sleep for the next day's sun.
I thought more sharply then of flowered death:
Of the friend's daughter in her pressed way,
Come upon her now in unexpected leaves,
Of words I would push forth, in surprise.
There is a permanence we seek.

Children of friends and others will be told,
In a useful fiction, that One lives above
The fixed fire of the stars at night.
Still, through distance and time's passage
Some pulse us light that we can see,
Though they are dead and air-combed coals.
The closing world runs, runs, and returns.
Nothing lives, nothing burns unconsumed.
Yet certain, shadowed through all our lives,
We hope for somewhere source, a bush of light.
There is a permanence we seek.

The Eagle & Phoenix Bridge

Columbus, Georgia

The New World that the desperate sailors found
Is no longer unmarked and innocent of ruins.
The bluffs of all slow rivers now
Bear old red mills whose
Long low shadows in the afternoon sun
Blacken the brownskin water.
No boys can downward raft in warmth,
Chilled in their passage again and again
By what is thrown by those looming walls
That lean above the banks.
Dark shapes angle sharp arrows that
Point and always down the seaward stream.

On a bridge that joins Georgia to another state,
I am drawn to draw aside
And drop keen-edged bricks upon the striped
Smooth river's muscular back,
But cross on to Alabama's pine green hills
Only more and more aware of how undyingly
The always shedding snake of time slides on.

Octave

A brother of the thinker Wittgenstein
I once read had one arm only
And a passion to play the piano.
He commissioned composers, therefore,
To write pieces for the left hand
And so died complete.
I, on the other,
Have found no one to arrange for me.

The Last Translation

*Rockville, Md.....Thirty years after the church denied him burial with
his ancestors in the cemetery of the Roman Catholic Church of St.
Mary's here, [F. Scott Fitzgerald] was laid to rest again with liturgical
ritual...in the Church cemetery.*
                    —*New York Times,* November 6, 1975

Time's lichens can cause thick granite to relent,
Altering at the end even the most adamant
By nothing more than the rising of sun upon sun.
(I count on this truth for reasons of my own.)
You cannot gaze upon copper domes gone green
Or climb stone steps with basins grooved and worn
By long dead feet and not believe it. Time's passage
Bears a gradual and conversionary message.

To earth outside a Maryland town a rotted
Body is carried across the road and added
With subdued solemnity, allowed at last
To enter the society of the parents' plot
By a Church that has changed its ways, if not its mind.

Small ceremony. Only the only daughter's hand
Sifts the Maryland dirt down. A priest not even born yet
When the last book came out reads a prayer and all depart.

The coffin is covered at length under a swell
On a Catholic cemetery's consecrated hill
That will be leveled soon by the quick thick lines
Of the long winter's erasing rains.
What does it matter, the skeptic spirit says,
Where the rough draft's waste paper finally lies?
Raised as this man was, I pray Latin still *ad rem:*
Dona Francisco, Domine, requiem.

from *By Poets Provoked* (1992)

Miss Lonelyhearts' Revenge

An obscure Miss
E. Dickinson
Once wrote off
For advice from
One of Boston's
Leading sages.

In Bartlett's book
He owns one line
While she alone
Holds title to
Five double-
Columned pages.

Autre Temps, Autre Moeurs

Just as you might, for a treat,
Drive the kids down to the seashore
To enjoy the waves,

The Dickinsons would sometimes ride
Emily out to the edge of town
To enjoy the graves.

Tabloid Retraction

When Emily Dickinson praised poetry that made her 'feel physically as if the top of my head were taken off,' she was calling for deeper endorphin payloads.
—Brad Leithauser, "The Confinement of Free Verse"

Miss Dickinson, interviewed
While weeding her small hyphen-
Ated garden on the lower slope
Of Mount Parnassus, Massachusetts,
Denied ever using or even condoning the use
Of endorphins at any time or in any mode.
"Much less," she added, in her
Characteristic Upper Case voice,
"Never, never would I—Employ
So ugly a—Word—as—Pay*load*."

A Pause in the Hunt

Dickey's is a cunning imagination, metaphoric enough to evade its exegetes.
—Harold Bloom

"Shitfire and hell," Big Jim muttered aloud,
Bare chest heaving as he leaned against a tree,
Looking back at the woods he'd broken through,
"Them goddamn exegetes, they're gainin' on me."

"I reckon," he drawled with a crooked grin,
"I know a way to evade them sons-a-whores."
So on he plunged, but squatted now and then
And left some strangely scented metaphors.

Imaginis Factor

Though California-born
Robert Frost was no fool.
He kept the engine of his old
4-Wheel Drive New England Persona
Tuned, turning over, and ticking—

Despite all those winters
That he spent out of the snow
In the Florida tropical sun
He never once published a single poem
Called "After Papaya Picking."

The Shropshire Lad Reflects On the Queerness of Life

If Mo Jackson 'ad not sailed away
If 'e'd given 'arf a sign,
We'd never 'ave 'ad *A Shropshire Lad*.
No, sir, not a bloody line.

But sail away 'e did, straight Mo
And never turned once 'is 'ead.
Poor mousy Alf, that Latin twit
Made Literature instead.

Housman at the Regattas

the alumni read the biographies

Come Spring, he would come to the races
In the most proper boater and tie.
He would come to the riverside races
To watch as the rowers rowed by.

We thought that he attended the races
For our sakes, to cheer on our side,
But, ah no, he attended those races
To savor a love that had died.

As a young man he'd loved a strong oarsman,
Though silent with love from afar.
As an old man—and honored—he joined us,
A veteran touching a scar.

On the bank as the bodies slid past him,
He remembered the love of his youth,
And then back in his bachelor chambers
He versified lies out of truth.

Through the years we have read all the poems,
Full of the bitterest rue.
Now, recalling his look at those races,
We nod and we murmur, "It's true."

First Edition, 1855

Before a man can make a poem, he must create a poet.
—Hayden Carruth

Ferried from Brooklyn
From Fulton to Broadway
Often he swaggered, often he came.
After a while
Everyone knew him,
Democratically Walt, not Walter, by name.

Sang songs of himself
As a yawper, a "rough,"
One with the drivers and singers on stage.
Hand-set his poems
And published himself
On many and many a free-flowing page.

Wrote of his glowing
Great loving nature,
Biblically making so manly a noise,
Few of his readers
Ever suspected
Most of that love was directed at boys.

Honor The Whitman,
Heap up his laurels
High as his Quakerly rosy-red ass.
Praise to that strider,
That omnibus rider,
That mower who mulched us such leavings of grass.

An Ould Hand at Coole Remembers

Ach, do I remember Yeats?
I remember him real well—
Thin, nearsighted, and as batty as
A tower with no bell.

What I most recall of him
Is how often he would try
To count them ould fat swans
Before they'd lift and fly.

I can hear still his high, thin voice
Counting 'em two by two.
He'd get up into the forties
When *Up!* the bastards flew.

Now this went on for weeks on end.
He'd count and off they'd soar.
He'd stand and shake his skinny fist
As they headed for the moor.

One day ould Lady Gregory
Who owned that House at Coole
Came up to me and said,
"I'm sick of the bloody fool.

"Go tie the legs of all them birds
And lay them in a line."
I did. And that's how he came up with
His number fifty-nine.

And there I stood all covered with
What frightened swans let go,
And all the silly clot could say,
Was "Naow at lahst I know."

Remember Yeats? Ach, sure I do.
How could a man forget?
Whenever I think of him and his poem
I smell that swanshit yet.

from *Scrimshaw: Quatrains and Clerihews* (1993)

QUATRAINS

Lamentation

They write the novels.
I write the rhymes.
They get the dollars.
I get the dimes.

Adult Education

I took a class in poetry.
My girlfriend threw a pot.
She makes a decent living
And I do not.

Blind Date

I courted Lady Luck.
I wined her and dined her.
I paid the check, looked up,
And couldn't find her.

Revisionist

I tell you Homer got it wrong.
I don't care what's in your tome.
The real war started when the hero said,
"Penelope, I'm home."

Discrimination

In the world of camels, I've no doubt,
A caste system's been worked out.
Camels with a single hump must rue
Consorting with the ones with two.

The Origins of the Art

I know why it is that poets cry
And why their hearts ache.
They know that every pen runs dry
And points of pencils break.

Taking the Cuts

Man's life is filled with ups and downs,
Of turn and turnabout:
Thirteen hundred and thirty times
George Herman Ruth struck out.

Esthetic Ethics

She walks in Beauty past me
In tight designer jeans.
Sometimes, it seems, the end
Does justify the means.

The Classless Society of Poetry

Keats, he was a guttersnipe—
George Gordon was a Lord:
The Muse, she is indifferent to
The pitcher, not the poured.

Translation

Loss in any tongue I know
Crosses over true:
Dit toujours le corbeau,
"Jamais, jamais plus."

Ordo Mundi

Order in this universe?
Finding some isn't hard:
Dewey's Decimal System and
The graves in a church's yard.

Winter Piece

We are never far from the world
That Brueghel painted in.
The children skate upon the ice
And still the ice is thin.

An Epigram for Halloween

One day of honesty
For life and all its lies—
Everyone is *openly*
Wearing a disguise.

CLERIHEWS

Michelangelo
Lunching on a single tangelo
Dropped down from the Sistine Ceiling
Both the pips and the peeling.

Mary Baker Eddy
Had a faith that was steady.
So certain was she of being healed,
She let lapse her Blue Cross and Blue Shield.

Edgar Allan Poe
After his tenth whiskey said, "Le'sh go.
There's a story I haven't finished yet,
Called *The Pindulum and the Pet*."

Percy Bysshe Shelley
Was never a Nervous Nellie.
He said, "Though the clouds are menacing and grey,
I'll go sailing anyway."

Sir Philip Sidney
Wrote some good things, didn't he?
I've always found especially nice
His cardiac advice.

from *The Ballads of Eskimo Nell and Others* (1995)

The Ballad of Margaret Mary

A Tale of the Old West

From movies you've seen you think you know
All the ways the West was won,
But I doubt you've heard the story of
The Schoolmarm and Her Gun.

Now back in the Eighteen-Eighties
Submissive women were the rule
When Margaret Mary McElroy
Left a Boston Convent School.

I have to pause a moment here
To set the record straight:
I said she *left* that Convent School.
In truth, she was shown the gate.

Ah, yes, kicked out was Margaret Mary,
Humiliatingly expelled
For certain views of The Female Sex
She obstinately held.

She thought in no uncertain terms
That "Woman Was *Not* Inferior."
What's worse, she said so right out loud
In front of Mother Superior.

Beneath her wimple that good nun's face
Reacted with a flinch.
She scurried off to confer with
The Pastor, Father Lynch.

Apprised of the girl's rebellion,
Father Lynch went to The Top.
The Cardinal saw in an instant
Such talk just had to stop.

His Eminence had a political heart
Beneath his crimson vest.
"I know what shall we do," he said.
"We'll ship her way out West."

The Cardinal pulled some strings and put
Margaret Mary on a train
That carried passengers westward
Across the fruited plain.

Are you surprised that Margaret Mary
Acquiesced in her exile?
Well, she did and went most willingly.
In fact, she wore a smile.

The Cardinal, quite by accident,
Had given her a career.
She faced The West and her teaching post
Without a trace of fear.

She knew that she could hold her own
Whatever came her way:
Under the undies in her portmanteau
An equalizer lay.

For Margaret Mary's father had been
(Before alcohol brought him down)
As fine a cop as had ever walked
A beat in Boston town.

He'd wanted a son, but got a girl—
A fact he couldn't change—
So week after week he'd taken her
With him to the pistol range,

And there the little red-haired lass,
With cotton firmly eared,
Had blasted targets all to shreds
As nearby cops all cheered.

By the time Margaret Mary reached
The state of womanhood
She was a better shot than her father
(And believe me he was good).

But booze, as it will, took its toll:
Dad's liver ceased to function.
Father Lynch was called and left the man
Oiled with Extreme Unction.

And so on his deathbed dear old Dad,
Half through sweet Heaven's door,
Bequeathed to his darling daughter
A Colt Navy .44.

Which legacy lay in the bottom of
Margaret Mary's travel bag
With a box of eighty bullets.
Wrapped in a linen rag.

Broken Jawbone, Arizona,
Was where she set up school.
She taught the children all three R's
Along with The Golden Rule.

Margaret Mary prospered and grew
In wisdom, age, and grace,
Making most of her friends among the girls
Who worked at Miss Kitty's place.

Oh, Tombstone, Dodge City, and Deadwood
Are locales of lawless fame,
But compared with Broken Jawbone
Those towns were teacup tame.

The man who controlled Broken Jawbone
Was known as Nevada Slim.
There wasn't a man in all the West
Who wasn't afraid of him.

He'd killed off a dozen sheriffs—
A couple of marshals, too.
In fact, someone always died each time
Slim went for his gun and drew.

The entire town lived in total fear
Except for a single one:
Margaret Mary made a careful point
Of keeping clean her gun.

One afternoon, her classes over,
Margaret Mary packed her books.
She left—and there stood Nevada Slim
With one of his evil looks.

"Schoolmarm," he said, "I been studyin' you
And you're lookin' mighty fine.
I've half a mind to lay you down
And make you truly mine."

"Why, Nevada Slim," Margaret Mary said
In a voice both coy and pert,
"What took you so long, you devil you?"
And she lifted up her skirt.

The gunfighter leered and licked his lips
As he saw a flash of thigh.
It was the final thing Nevada saw
With his lascivious eye—

For Margaret Mary had calmly drawn
From a holster on her calf
The Colt .44 she used to blast
Nevada's head in half.

From that day on she was famous
From Canada down to Texas
For proving in her own proud way
How equal are the sexes.

And what became of her? Did she find
Love and life and laughter?
Of *course* she did. Miss Kitty and she
Lived happily ever after.

The Ballad of Shanghai Sally

A Tale of Old Manhattan

Oh, many were the bawdy houses
Along The Bowery's alleys,
But none was bawdier than the one
Known as Shanghai Sally's.

Now Shanghai Sally was not Chinese
(Though many are in New York).
She'd been baptized Sara Kelly
Back home in County Cork.

But driven across the seas she'd been
When the potatoes failed,
And on her second night On The Town
The Kelly girl was jailed.

And there in the Women's Section
Of that Place of Servitude
Young Sara learned some Lessons in Life
That were both raw and crude.

When she was out on the street again,
She'd vowed she'd not be poor,
And she set her goal to own a House
With a Red Light by the door.

She saved and scrimped, she scrimped and saved,
Her dollars mounted high,
Till one day she tapped an Investor Man
As he was passing by.

"Kind sir," she said in a lilting brogue,
"I'd like to start A Place."
Perceiving a profit, the Investor Man
Fixed a smile on his face.

A shrewd Man of Commerce he was.
He gave her a searching look.
Then he nodded and said, "I'll listen, my dear
Now what's *your* Special Hook?"

"Oh sir, kind sir, I've thought and thought
An awful lot about it.
I know I must distinguish my House.
I know it—do not doubt it—

"And here's The Pitch that I've developed:
I know *The Strange* excites.
A man searches for exotic things
When seeking his delights

"And so I've chosen to call my Place
Where lustful men may dally
The Oriental House of Sin—
Proprietor: Shanghai Sally."

"That's it!" the Investor Man cried out
And gave her cheek a peck
And on the spot he wrote for her
A many-zeroed check.

I need not tell you what followed then—
You're bright and you can guess—
The Oriental House of Sin
Was an Overnight Success.

Oh, week after week the money taken
Made an outrageous tally,
And rich and famous grew the Madam
Known as Shanghai Sally.

But there's never been a Paradise
Not furnished with a Snake.
Sally's was a Vice Cop who refused
To join others On The Take.

The Detective's name, of course, was
An Irish one, Joe Flynn,
Who had set his holy heart upon
Closing Sally's House of Sin.

Now Joe had been an Altar Boy.
He loved the Lord his God,
And took his work more seriously
Than others on The Squad.

Joe had learned in Parochial School
This World's a Tearful Valley.
He morally worked without remorse
To shut down Shanghai Sally.

And thus it chanced One Fateful Night
They met at Fourth and Water:
The Pure Detective, chaste and cold,
And Satan's Favorite Daughter.

And what befell? You can look it up:
Shanghai Sally's House of Sin
Showed thereafter on The City's Rolls
As owned by Mrs. Flynn.

from *Nominal Verse: Clerihews* (1998)

Saint Thomas Aquinas
Troubled by a runny sinus
Said to Saint Albert the Great,
"You godda Kleenex, mate?"

Aristotle
Was not polyglottal.
The only language he could speak
Was Greek.

Alexander Graham Bell
Deserves a place in nethermost Hell
For giving telemarketers the awful power
To call at one's dinner hour.

William Blake
Refused to eat Angel Cake.
It is not recorded if he eschewed
Devil's Food.

Anne Boleyn
Was pretty good at sin.
In fact for cheating on him Henry said,
"Off with her head."

Clare Boothe
About the War of the Sexes wrote the truth.
Then she entered into a truce
By marrying Mr. Luce.

Tyrus Cobb
Was basically pretty good at his job.
In a business based on changing places,
He grew rich by stealing bases.

René Descartes
At cogitation was exceptionally smart.
He took for his *point d'appui*
"Je pense, donc je suis."

John Donne
Was never much fun.
In fact, the phrase *metaphysically grim*
Pretty much captures him.

Richard D'Oyly Carte
Said to Gilbert and Sullivan, "Bill, Art,
Act One of *Pinafore's* running rather long.
Can't we cut a patter song?"

Maud Gonne
In her stocking feet stood six foot one.
When William Yeats proposed that they wed,
High above his, she shook her head.

Ernest Hemingway
Never acted in a lemming way.
In a war or on the hunt,
He made sure to be in front.

Henry James
Had a duality of Christian names,
Which is true of many another:
For example, his brother.

John Fitzgerald Kennedy
Deserves a limerick, not a threnody.
Before the fell assassin's fatal shot
Jack fooled around a lot.

Francis Scott Key
Made it hard for you and me
To sing in any satisfactory manner
"The Star-Spangled Banner."

John Knox
Never bothered with alarm clocks.
He knew it was his predestined fate
Never to rise late.

David Herbert Lawrence
In his own time was held in abhorrence
But is latterly
Greatly admired for his Lady Chatterley.

Franz Liszt
At fifty-five became a priest
(A tricky rhyme you may have missed
If you pronounce his name as "List").

Claude Monet
Weary of painting stacks of hay
Turned to turning out scads and scads
Of lily pads.

Friedrich Nietzsche
Found this world somewhat less than peachy.
In fact, ordinary life for him
Was pretty grim.

Sylvia Plath
Was not overly given to math
Except for her lifelong attraction
To the skill of self-subtraction.

Hester Prynne
Lettered in Varsity Sin.
She was legend in her day
Walking though Salem with her big red A.

Theo van Gogh
Sent his brother some extra dough.
With it Vincent bought canvas, paint, beer,
And a bandage for his ear.

William Butler Yeats
Never rode on roller skates.
When it comes to a motor scooter,
The question is mooter.

from *The Jerusalem Rooster* (2001)

Iskariotes

I have handled these coins in every possible way.
I have heaped them up in all their combinations:
Ten piles of three—three piles of ten—
I have even towered them thirty high,
And then, with an idle fingertip, toppled them.
I have bagged them up and poured them out again.

In the April night air, the upper room grows chill.
I am alone now, the others gone to the garden.
I can play publican on the long table made of pine,
Stacking and stacking my coins on the rough boards
That had been linen-covered earlier when I whispered,
"Is it I?" and swallowed the bread and the blood-red wine.

I clink my silver over and over in moonlit circles
And wonder at the cunning of my new masters—
How did they know that it would all come down to this:
My sitting here in this cold, dark room, troubled,
Awaiting my own time to go out to the garden
And give the sign they demanded of me—that kiss?

The Jerusalem Rooster

No common cock of the walk in the High Priest's courtyard,
I paid attention when the rabbis argued Scripture and the Law.
I know the lesson of *The Book of Jonah*—I know how ill
Yahweh treats reluctant prophets. It stuck in my yellow craw,

But when the Angel of the Lord appeared with his command
About Simon Peter, I made a vow that I would do my best.
Although I did not like being used, I agreed to play
My part, but with a drooping tail and a lowered crest.

It was not easy keeping clear of all those serving maids,
Each one ready to wring my neck and, after draining me dry,
Toss me in a pot of soup. I dodged their dirty feet all night
Following Peter, listening closely for his, "I deny."

And then, at dawn, denial arrived, three times in fact:
Galilean curses declaring, *I never knew him!*
Betrayal came as prophesied, and so—as ordered—
I swelled and sent the keen sword of my cry right through him.

From the Cyrenaic

Him they wanted dead, of course, but not yet—
His life to end, but only at their end,
Not on the way, not on a narrow street's stones,
But high on the hill outside the city gate
Where all could see and be given a lesson.
I need not tell you how tall the centurion was.
They are all huge men, those Roman soldiers.
I watched as the prisoner for the third time
Fell face down under the heavy cross's arm
And saw the officer look over the lookers-on.
I sensed the man's thoughts and began to shrink,
But he spied me—how could he not?——in the crowd,
And pointing me out with his baton said,
"*Tu, Negre.*" I hunched my shoulders and brought
My right hand curling inward to my breast.
I was still saying in gesture, in dumb show,
"Who, me, Captain?" when one of his legionnaires
Hooked me by the upper arn, dragged me forward,
Cuffed my head, and made me take up the beam,
Fit it to my shoulder's hollow, and stumble forward.

Come to Jerusalem that morning on business,
I curse my ill-fortune at being on that street,
For pausing to take in the spectacle,
For being in the wrong place at the wrong time,
But most of all for being born with so ebon a skin.
No further falls for him the rest of the way
To the hill where at last I could drop the load.
I had seen nothing of him all along the march
Save the bloody back of his once-white robe,
But then, for an instant only, he turned his face,
And in his sad eyes I saw a flash of thanks
To me for sharing his burden, for taking,
Even against my will, a part of his punishment.
Shoved aside by the soldiers, I shrank back

To the edge of the crowd and stayed to the end.
Yes, I have heard what his followers are saying:
That he was a prophet and more, that he rose
After the Sabbath Day from the dead. Perhaps.
But I know, better than any disciple of his,
How hard, heavy, and *final* felt that wood.

Veteranus Loquitur

It was no picnic on the *Campagna,* I tell you,
Serving out there in the deserts of Judaea—
Those damned by the gods stubborn pigheaded Jews
Just didn't know how to knuckle under
And act like a decent occupied nation.

If I had some silver for all the gobs I dodged
Or for the stones I clanged away with my shield
(Oh, those Jews were great ones for rocks and spit),
I'd be retired in a villa near Lake Como drinking wine,
Being well-serviced by Numidian slave girls.

There was, though, one good thing about that tour:
Being assigned to the special execution squads,
A man got some great experience out there.
Since the locals weren't allowed the death penalty.
We planted ourselves a forest of timber crosses,

But, like all good things, it got to be so routine
That the officers started to look the other way,
Letting the boys have some fun, if you get my drift.
The only rule was that the poor bastard
Had to be still alive when we topped the *tau.*

I don't have to tell you that some of the troops
Got out of control, what with whips and boots.
The worst were those two-legged sewer rats
Recruited out of the Capitoline slums.
Compared to them, the Gauls were schoolgirls.

One of the worst times I remember out there
Was when we pulled the assignment to nail up
Some meek little rabbi the procurator, Pilate—
That two-a-penny pussy-faced politician—
Called King of the Jews when he passed sentence.

The Fourth Squad turned into total apes that day.
Some joker rigged up a crown of spiky thorns
And wrapped up the man in a ragged castoff purple robe.
What stopped the clowning was the day: Sabbath Eve.
By Jewish Law the man had to be dead by sundown.

Come three o'clock, I was the *misericordia* man.
I took my field lance and drove it up and under
The armpit just like it says in the manual.
That did it, I can tell you—blood and water
Ran down my arm, red and wet and warm.

Three days later a rumor ran through all the garrison
That the man—get this—*had risen from the dead*!
Listen, if that poor son of a bitch made it back from Dis,
He came home with a hole in the side wide enough
To put your bloody hand in and touch his beating heart.

from *The Old Formalist* (2003)

The Old Formalist Considers The Tools of His Trade

They are truly paragons of patience itself,
My pens and pencils racked in an old coffee cup.
Night after night they stand, attentive as angels,
Hoping I will sit down, reach out, and take one up.

They contain within their rigid plastic or cedar bodies
Tubes of slow-drying ink or veins of semi-soft lead,
Ready to put down on any paper I have at hand
Whatever words I may draw from heart or head.

They stay still, but gathered like a stand of trees
Awaiting the saw, yearning for my selection.
Miltonic, mute as any in a grave by Gray,
They wait docilely my giving them their soul's direction.

Godlike, my hand hovers over their dark abyss.
Then chooses one for—ah—no better a verse than this.

The Old Formalist Mows His Lawn

I recall Whitman's child asking, "What is the grass?"
I can tell him what it is: it's a pain in the ass.

The Old Formalist Reads the Latest Quarterly

The articles, essays, and reviews are written
In a sturdy, workmanlike prose.
And the poems that are printed in these pages?
Ah—so are, so are those.

The Old Formalist Buys an iMac

Not employing pen and paper,
But keyboard, mouse, and screen
Does not make it any easier
To make your meanings mean.

The Old Formalist Reads a Sesquipedalian Poet

He seems to think the longer word the better.
This makes me a non-admirer.
I'd bet he'd go and call a *woolen sweater*
A *lanacious perspirer*.

The Old Formalist Reads the Annual "Best of" Anthology

Over the lines of too many poems
My eyes and mind have drifted.
All too often, the same conclusion:
Nothing in the sieve, nothing sifted.

The Old Formalist Tries to Balance His Checkbook

When it comes to mathematics,
I am Lee at Appomattox.

The Old Formalist Thinks About Couplets

I watch lovers unable not to nudge and touch
And think how I once was one of a pair of such.

The Old Formalist Contemplates the Returned SASE

On every misfortune the wise man
Puts a positive, optimistic take.
What marvelous bookmarks rejection slips
From *Poetry Magazine* make.

The Old Formalist Late at Night

Over such a blank white paper as this
Have they all hovered, my betters,
Working their missionary plodding way
In the wilderness of letters.

I am this night again at one with them,
Brothered by this unblemished sheet:
Auden's artful forms, Eliot's pious verse,
Emily's cold New England heat.

I recognize in this clean austere page
How superior is the company I keep.
I sigh. Then click my pen to close its flow
And turn myself to bed and sleep.

The Old Formalist Thinks of His Own Irish Wake

I will not smile. I will not wink.
I will not sip a single drink.

I will not dance. I will not sing.
I will not do a goddamned thing.

I will not mind. I will not care.
I will not be what's lying there.

from *Subscriptions: Epigraphical Verse* (2005)

Translated from the Attic

*Greek statues...are a reproach to common humanity. They seem to
have no sympathy with us, and not to want our admiration.*
—William Hazlitt on the Elgin Marbles

Do you think they suppose we really *like*
Standing around day after dreary day
In these cold and drafty museum halls,
While crowds of *hoi polloi* go slowly by,
Pretending not to be taking sidelong looks
At our tits and our pricks and our marbly balls?

Do you think they suppose we really *like*
Having always to be the cynosure
Of ten thousand probing prurient eyes
While the pornophilic minds behind them,
Despite all their aesthetic homilies,
Are making technical notes about our size?

These monotheistic barbarian
Repressed northern and neurotic
Fog-begotten sons of frigid English bitches,
Do you suppose they think we really *like*
Hanging about here in the altogether
With never a hint of bras nor breeches?

O, if only a god would come and break
This classical spell of ours, how swiftly
Back to sunny Greece they'd see us rise and fly,
Flashing them selenically one final
Fleeting glimpse of the perfectly dimpled
Demi-globes of our glistening *glutei*!

The Grammarian at the Dockside Pub

Dryden boasted that he 'would be glad to learn something about language from sailors'.
                                    —Owen Barfield, *Poetic Diction*

'E stands me to a pint like a right shipmate.
I figures 'e deserves to be set straight,
So I teaches the poor dumb son of a bitch
'Ow to distinguish between *that* and *which*.

Cultural Exchange

At Highgate school...[T. S. Eliot] tried to teach the smaller boys baseball, but it was not a success.
                                    —Peter Ackroyd, *T.S. Eliot: A Life*

This tapering tubular column, my lads,
Is called a *bat*. (One must use the proper term.)
And the ball is this albinated spheroid
Encapsulated by equine epiderm.

Let us survey the topography of the field,
An Objective Correlative of the game.
The book-bags I have placed will be our bases,
Giving the sport its eponymous name.

What are you murmuring, you there in the back row?
Yes, you Betjeman. You're the one I heard.
Speak up, boy, Share the joke with your classmates.
Silence, is it? Good. Not another word.

Master Betjeman permitting, I shall resume.
Where I stand is *home plate*, not the *wicket*.
Having struck the ball, one runs from base to base,
Not back and forth as one does in cricket.

Giggles again, Betjeman? You, too, Stetson?
Oh, all right, you devils. It's perfectly clear
I'm wasting my time. Go and play your soccer—
Or *football* as you all so malaprop it here.

It's Quicker

It [alcohol] is in fact the great exciter of the yes function in man.
—William James

Oh yes, yes indeed, William,
That's very, very true,
And, as Ogden Nash pointed out,
In *woman*, too.

Mrs. Melville

*Herman has taken to writing poetry. You need not tell anyone, for you
know how these things get around.*
—Elizabeth Shaw Melville in a letter, 1859

My Herman's taken to poetry writing,
But please don't tell a soul about it.
With rolling eyes and pen-point biting,
Yes, Herman's taken to poetry writing.
He fills the house with loud reciting.
(Oh, how I wish he would not shout it.)
Poor Herman's taken to poetry writing,
But please don't tell a soul about it.

Pet-Sitting

Emma took a month's holiday at Calais...leaving Hardy at Max Gate to cope with the cats, Markie, Snowdove, Pixie, and Comfy.
—Robert Gittings, Thomas Hardy's Later Years

Missing you, Emma, I prowl Max Gate—
Cold, irritable, and quite harumphy,
Trying to cope here with all of your cats:
Markie, Snowdove, Pixie, and Comfy.

Oh, yes—I cower here at old Max Gate
Subject to a sovereign felinarchy
Under the rule of all your cats:
Pixie, Comfy, Snowdove, and Markie.

How glad I am that we haven't another
With a name such as, say, Trixie,
As I contend here with all of your cats:
Comfy, Snowdove, Markie, and Pixie.

And so, from the back fence of Max Gate,
With Markie, Pixie, Comfy, and Snowdove,
I make a long meow to you in Calais:
Come home, please—and don't be slow, Love.

Remora

The future of criticism depends on the future of the other literary arts.
—Malcolm Cowley, American Perspectives #5

Absolutely correct, Malcolm,
Dead on and perfectly right:
Without a host to feed upon,
What good's a parasite?

from *Quatrains* (2010)

At Sea

Young, you think life is a cruise,
A pleasant vacation trip.
Old, you find that it's a voyage
On a Herman Melville ship.

Bipolar

On my head some dull days I feel
A soft depression dropping down.
When I gaze at the fence's other side,
The grass looks equally brown.

Cardiology

What stress induced Lowell's heart attack?
Perhaps it was his publisher's math
Which proved that he was being outsold
By the poems of Sylvia Plath.

Displacement

Sleep has a role in mental health.
Out of it sanity streams.
Each night we all go crazy
In the asylum of our dreams.

Economics 101

Between the very rich and the very poor
Lies a fundamental difference underneath:
The very rich are the ones who'll be buried
With perfectly straightened teeth.

Footnote to the Proverb

Walk a mile in the other man's shoes
To get an empathetic fix,
But don't do this if your size is ten
And his is only six.

Foresight

Aldous Huxley displayed once and for all
The professional writer's mind:
He began to practice typing in the dark
When told he was going blind.

George M. Koan

I asked my father, my first Zen master,
"What is the sound of one hand clapping?"
The next thing I recall hearing was
His right palm on my left ear, slapping.

Going, Going...Gone

The real World of Art?
Let me clue you in:
When the painter dies,
The auctioneers grin.

Jamais Plus

Poor Eddie Poe. Even after death
Into his works the monkey wrench:
He wound up in that corner of Heaven
Where all they speak is French.

Law Enforcer

X.J. Kennedy is a poet
To whom I'm totally partial.
He should be issued a silver badge
Naming him a U.S. Martial.

Making the Best

One brings what one can
To life's long struggle:
A man with just one hand
Must somehow learn to juggle.

Misfortune Cookie

Do not let a sense of security
Lull you and drug you.
You will meet a tall dark stranger—
And he will mug you.

On Digital Clocks

Technology serves us all,
Even the mentally sick.
A time bomb in a package
No longer needs to tick.

Plot Twist

With my luck, when my life is done,
Over and complete,
My headstone will very likely
Stand above my feet.

Portrait D'Artiste

James Joyce, ever continental,
To the end of his days
Pronounced his novel's title as
Oo-liss-ayze.

Quest

When I was young I went in search
Of the holiest Holy Grail.
Now I'd be happy just to find
Fewer bills among my mail.

The Thickets of the Law

Have you ever noticed how
In the middle of the word distress
There lurk three awful letters:
I and *R* and *S* ?

Tuition

My first lesson in deception?
I learned it as a kid
When a young girl said to me,
"Let's not and say we did."

Via Negativa

Think of a ladder.
Think of a net.
Mostly nothing,
But something yet.

Whitman, Thou Shouldst Be Living At This Hour

O, my profligate America!
So many acres of grass set aside
For those who play golf
And those who have died.

from *Quadrivia* (2012)

A Metaphor for Irony

A metaphor for irony?
Nothing simpler, nothing neater:
Having diabetes makes
One's ice cream all the sweeter.

Death's Casino...

Leaves nothing to chance.
It cheats and cheats with zeal:
Marked is every deck of cards
And rigged is its roulette wheel.

Depositum Fidei

I am an obscure meagerly published poet
And often recount when slightly drunk
How Emily Dickinson squirreled away her poems
In Maggie Maher's trunk.

Dichtung und Wahrheit

In the cold black German night
As the cattle cars rolled by
Many a crossing guard, I think,
Hummed Heine's "Lorelei."

Education

During my long years of schooling
What did I study most of all?
Minute by minute in every class
The clock on the classroom wall.

From the Yardarm

Let us all when our death
Comes finally near
Say, "God bless..." whoever
Is *our* Captain Vere.

Imminent Foreclosure

Young I chose to live in a tower.
Yes, of ivory it was made.
Old I learn there's a mortgage on it
And, yes, it must be paid.

Intimations of Mortality

I am traveling steerage in a liner
Far out on a northern sea.
Overhead I hear the orchestra practicing
"Nearer My God to Thee."

Keeping Up with the Oops

Conspicuous consumption is a human constant,
A fact paleontology reveals.
Even prehistoric man wanted wider caves,
Thicker clubs, and bigger, rounder wheels.

Late 20th Century Question

Will the future students
Learning about their betters
Study volumes whose titles begin
The Life and E-Mail Letters...?

Liquefiction

Be careful when you read the poets.
Their work's designed to fool ya.
Never once in all his life did Herrick
Possess a girl named Julia.

November Verse

Late autumn and
The leaves are leaving
And little children are
Runny noses sleeving.

On Optimism

Oh, obstinate is all human hope
Upon this dismal earth.
Even the undertaker's wife
Keeps on giving birth.

On the Internet

Twenty minutes
With the poetry bloggers
And I am ready
For a dozen lagers.

The Old Adam

Each man assembles his own Eden
And gives each animal a name.
My Paradise differs from yours,
But our Serpent is the same.

Thus I Refute It...

The Old Philosopher wondered,
"The Objective World, is it real?"
Just before he stepped upon
A discarded banana peel.

Underclassman

Young people keep calling me a Senior.
Nearly deaf, I yet hear them loud and clear.
Still, somewhere in my soul I am convinced
I've only started on my Freshman year.

Variation on an Old Adage

In my long passage through life
I've learned at least one thing:
In this wide world of the half-assed
The total ass is king.

Victorian Romance

Did Robert Browning as he fell down
To propose on one of his knees
Realize that along with Liz
Came Flush and all those fleas?

Wistful Thinking

I sometimes wish America's
Knowledge of Poetry was ampler:
Say "Whitman" to the Average Joe
And his first thought is "Sampler."

from *Harrington's Couplets* (2013)

A Question of Linguistics

If we call those persons who live
In the sad state of mania
Maniacs,

Why then do we not call those people
Who live to the west of New Jersey
Pennsylvaniacs?

After a Lecture at Emory University

The Buddhist scholar who'd talked for an hour
About nothingness and the emptiness of death
And the old joke of the sound of the One Hand Clap

Climbed into my built-by-Asians Nissan
And buckled the passenger side seat belt
With a decisive Occidental and Christian *snap!*

An Earlier Sunday Morning

Under the echoes of old bronze Lutheran bells
Solid burghers of Reading, Pennsylvania,
On the way home from church to breakfasts
Of scrapple, eggs, and toast—each wife behind
By a pace as befitted her place as *die Frau—*

Nodded to where, on vacation from Harvard,
The son of Lawyer Stevens rocked on the porch,
Picking out on his mind's blue ukulele
Tuneful new hymns as he sang to himself
"Tinka tanka tunk" and "Hoobla hoobla how."

At Home Depot

Knowing my luck, if I had been Noah,
Given the Lord's warning
Of the impending downpour

I would have built the ark in my basement
Exactly one cubit wider
Than my narrow cellar door.

Dear Elizabeth Bishop

I'm sorry to have to report
Your old filling station's gone.
Nowadays we're forced
To pump the gas ourselves—

And your serried, sighing
Cans of oil? Ah, now they urge
EXXON—ON—ON—ON
As they're ranked upon the shelves.

Improvisation

I watched a boy sliding downhill
On a day of rare Atlanta snow
Using for his sled a trash can lid—

And remembered how long years ago
Poor and miles away north of here
It was the sort of thing I once did.

Like the Roman Roads

All Interstates and *Autobahns*
With their wide straightaways and inter-
Secting, overpassing loops

Were originally, let us never forget,
Designed by *Wehrmacht* and Pentagon
For the swift moving of tanks and troops.

On the Death of a Typographer

for Chuck Robertson (1926-2000)

No one I ever knew
Believed more than he
In the afterlife, in a world beyond,

So I pray him in Heaven
With his heroes:
Janson, Baskerville, Garamond.

On the Habit of Verse

Writing verse is like the proverb
About the drinking of wine,
Apt and perfectly true:

First you write the verse,
Then the verse writes the verse,
And finally the verse writes you.

Sic Transit

Ah, flickering and fleeting
Like a firefly's flight in the night
Is all earthly power and fame.

At John Kennedy's graveside
Cardinal Cushing's aspergil
Put out The Eternal Flame.

The Journey

Downriver it is all, of course, dash—
Pennants in the wind and the whistle-scream.
The swift water runs, and we with it, seaward
Like lovers in a wild waltzing dance.

Upriver, though, it is all an ugliness:
A bumbling slow strive, a steady slog.
Still, to batter a low bow-wave before us—
That is truly, in truth, to advance.

Traduttore

Translation is hard. It is not like
Pouring water from pitcher to pitcher
Or sunlight passing through a pane.

Consider the early computer
That rendered *Out of sight, out of mind*
As *Invisibly insane.*

from *Ms. Muse & Me* (2013)

Ms. Muse after a Poetry Reading

Ms. Muse burst into my room and slammed the door,
A sure sign that she was well and truly pissed off.
"I was just at a so-called poetry reading," she said.
"The son of a bitch should have been hissed off."

"That bad?' I said, glad she was mad at someone else.
She answered, "Not only was each piece a jumble,
Full of obscure references and prosiness,
He recited every damned one in a monotone mumble."

Then she broke into French as she sometimes does,
"*Ou sont les lecteurs d'antan?* Richard Burton,
Dylan Thomas—guys like that delivered lines
With the majestic voice of Oz behind the curtain.

"Look, I know readings are important for you poets,
A chance to thrill blue-haired ladies, sell some books,
But why are so many of them like going to a restaurant
With menus dreamed up by inadequate, amateur cooks?

"Things weren't like that in the good old days back in Greece
When Homer was on stage playing his acoustic lyre.
I tell you those readings really rocked. The crowds
At the Athens East Amphitheater were always on fire.

"Ever since then things have gone friggin' downhill—
You know the direction: from truly bad to truly worse.
Why can't you goddamned poets get tape recorders
And stand in front of mirrors and rehearse?"

I knew she was winding down when she started
Murmuring, "It's enough to make a Greek girl weep."
I poured her a couple of warm Buds and eventually
She slowly calmed down and fell asleep.

Ms. Muse on Matrimony

Poets should *not* marry poets.
Think of Sylvia and Ted:
Both of them in competition
Even with one of them dead.

Ms. Muse Brags a Little

One of my proudest achievements was when
I lodged this thought in Emily's head:
"Take every freakin' comma out
And use the *dash* instead."

Ms. Muse Inspires a Drinking Song

Ms. Muse, she said to me,
"No poems for you tonight.
You're too far gone in booze
Properly to write."

"Oh, yeah?" I cried aloud.
I'll show you what I think."
Then I dipped my pen in gin
And sipped another ink.

Ms. Muse on Writers' Conferences

Every blooming spring and summer
The same old games get themselves played:
Wannabe poets sniffing around me,
Hoping to get themselves laid.

Ms. Muse Sips a Latte

Ms. Muse sat with me in a Starbucks
And reminisced about the good old days.
Telling me tales of her many adulteries
With the likes of Donne and Chaucer.

At one point she looked up and said,
"Christ, at these prices you'd think
They'd serve the goddamned Joe
In a Wedgwood cup and saucer."

Ms. Muse Chats with The Old Formalist

I'm happy you've gone and become
A geezer, you dithering old fart.
We lose too many damned young ones
At the very beginning of their art,

Though I'll admit it's awfully hard
To think of Jack Keats surviving Rome
Only to wind up in a wheelchair
At the Mount Parnassus Nursing Home.

Ms. Muse Asks a Literary Question

If Poetry is irrelevant—
One of Kulchur's
Oldest rants and recitals—

Why do novelists
Keep raiding anthologies
In search of better titles?

from *Sundries* (2014)

Among My Hopes

If alphabetized in Heaven are the streets
Happily will I visit Avenue K
To hear what Kierkegaard and Keats
Eternally have to say.

A Proverbial Truth

Disability is no laughing matter.
It is not a fit subject for the jocular.
Still, in the country of the blind,
It pays to be uniocular.

At Ford's Theater

Think of that poor cast—
Not one curtain call
The night John Booth
Upstaged them all.

At Walter Reed

When you list all those who profit
From war and war's loud alarms
Be sure to include the providers
Of prosthetic legs and arms.

Carpenter

I'll tell you some truth
If have some you must:
You cannot saw wood
And not produce dust.

Chasing the Long Ball

We are all outfielders on the run
Across the green grass, looking back,
Hoping to hear our cleated feet
Crunch in time on the warning track.

Clerihew: Bierce

Ambrose Bierce
Wrote prose both funny and fierce.
Despite the fame of him,
No one knows whatever became of him.

Coffee Spooner

One night I heard myself slurring
The *veritas* that is in *vino,*
So I tried to sober myself up
With a cap of cuppacino.

Elegy for Heaney

The thumb and forefinger part,
No longer one.
The squat pen falls to earth.
The digging's done.

Failed Arsonist

I am, I am, sad to say
An inveterate small versifier:
Thousands of tiny flint/steel sparks
And never a four alarm fire.

Freudian

There is always a hidden meaning
In the things that parents do.
They are teaching their babies death
When they play at Peek-a-Boo.

In Praise of Adverbs

Words only for enhancing other words
That work like the dots of white
Painters put in the portrait sitter's eye
Surely to suggest the light.

Lady Luck

I sat across the table from her,
My chin upon my fist.
She had a Rolex on her mind.
I had a Timex on my wrist

Lessons

My father in his playful way
Taught me many useful things.
I learned that *nothing's certain* when
He laid his aces on my kings.

Mission

This is the destiny of Eve's
Every son and daughter:
To be sent out with a sieve,
Commanded to gather water.

On the Cinder Track

In the race against Time
I'm hopelessly outclassed.
I've noticed lately even
My watch is running fast.

Pessimist

When all you have is a sack of dust
After years and years of mining,
Remember the truth I told you trust:
Every cloud has a pewter lining.

Political Advice

Stand neither to the left or right.
Stay firmly in the middle.
Note how Rome is always burning.
Learn to play the fiddle.

Purgatory

Dante knew there was a station
On the subway before Heaven.
After Confession, after Absolution,
A Penance is always given.

Serenity Prayer

When I am troubled by the Mill of Life's daily grind—
The irritations of its low, annoying hum—
I bring the words of St. Francis softly to mind:
"Dear Lord, where is all this birdshit coming from?"

Subterfuges

Nature is truly deceptive,
Filled with cunning lies:
Think of spiders spinning nets
For acrobatic flies.

Sunshine State

Poor Florida child,
Sadly never to know
The holy moment when
Rain turns into snow.

The Loneliness of the Long Distance Leader

Does the proud lead Canada gander flying south
Ever have a doubt enter his anserine mind
And be moved to crane his neck around
To check if there are others still behind?

To a Critic

You say my verse is too thin—
My thought a shallow muddle.
I say the sky can be reflected
Very well in a pavement's puddle.

Tremors

Hurricanes, tornadoes, and earthquakes:
How often the news we get is grim.
Nature sometimes shakes us off like water
From a Labrador after a swim.

Unclipped

I have a sure measure of Time.
Unlike my watch it never fails:
The accumulation of grime
Under the edges of my nails.

You, Otis Redenbacher

The sum of all my wisdom?
I say it with a sigh.
At the bottom of all popcorn urns
Unopened kernels lie.

Clerihew: Frost

Elinor Frost
As a girl never reckoned the cost
Of taking on such a terrible job:
Living with Rob.

Uncollected Verse

Falling Back in Standard Time

November lamplighter, I make my rounds
To retrieve again the hour that was lost
On purpose late one night the spring before
And discover again how few are the clocks
I own, not one of them not electric.

On my way I find other vanished hours.
Recalling how my orderly father would—
Home from the hurried Sunday Mass at noon—
Set anew for the coming seven days
The family's mastering Seth Thomas clock:

How he would take in his hand the sacred key
None of his children was allowed to touch
And open the brass-rimmed hinged glass cover
Of the clock's face as the priest had earlier
The tabernacle filled with the Substance of Christ.

He then would wind and wind until he felt
A firm resistance in his hand that said
Even regulation has its limit.
That hand is dead now and can no longer
Turn at all to any measure of time.

I continue in my own slow circuit
Among the numerals of my alarm,
Microwave, cable-box, and VCR.
Breaking the current, I see them all blinking
As though surprised as I by time reversed.

Stasis

Rowing into a suddenly risen
Late April afternoon's thunderstorm
The eight with slow small motions
Of their oars against the river's
Sluggish down-pulling current
Hold their shell unmoving
Under the dark deep crescent
Blackstone arch of a railroad bridge,
Sheltering themselves from,
Paradoxically, the slashing rain,
The source of the very element
That keeps their craft suspended.
    Oh, I was such a rower once.

Resting in their pull upriver,
The oarsmen are in a condition
Like the ones the nuns in Catechism
Called The State of Sanctifying
Grace, in which you were, even
As a child, required to desire to be
At the unimaginable hour of your death,
The world on all sides erupting
With loud satanic explosions,
While your soul safely rested
Under an angel's wing, still
In the serenity of its innocence.
    Oh, I was such a rester once.

After My Mother's Funeral Mass

Outside the parish church of my boyhood,
Waiting for the undertaker's hired hands
To work the coffin down the steep steps
Into the back of the idling hearse,
I sat in a car lined up with all the others
For the long slow ride to the cemetery.

Through sunlight wincing off windshields
I watched children from my parochial school
At play on the church's parking lot,
Too poor to have the public school's grass,
And I knew I would never again be so close
To the mysterious sources of my soul's arising—

The church where once I called on God
And dreamed that I was called in turn,
The school where under the eyes of nuns
I learned to read, write, and do numbers,
But, most important of all, that now dead body
Beneath whose heart my own heart was formed.

Then, without a second's warning, the very flesh
She had given form and life to rebelled,
And there rose through my lungs, throat,
And mouth a spasm of inconsolable sobbing
As I became again what I suddenly saw there:
A small boy fallen on the world's black asphalt.

Anamnesis

Remembering my brother's wake,
I remember my father's wake
At which my brother said to me
(And to a brother in law, himself
In the time between the wakes, dead)
How well his life was going, and yet
He wondered just how soon would come
The time for him to bear his cross,
Proving how closely he had listened,
As all of his father's children had,
To the nuns of his boyhood's school.

And soon thereafter it began:
A child's death by drowning, a stroke
That separated his mind from speech
And ended his smooth career of words,
Followed at last by the quick cancer
That he characteristically,
Funny and brave and stammering,
After talk of baseball and politics,
During my last telephone call to him,
Declared that he would beat. He did not.

And now with another wake to remember,
I remember the presence of his children
Over whom I know he'd anguished
Through more than one long dark night.
They had each, I saw, in the years
I had not seen, gone from being
Little children to full adulthood.

I watched as they faced a father's death
With a faintly humorous faith
So like his own he would have wept
As I did with them the next day
At what was, when I was their age,
A Solemn High Mass for the Dead,
When the priest wore black instead of white
And the choir sang in Latin "O Day of Wrath."
The liturgy changes. Death does not.

The Schuylkill in Flood

circa 1954

Not quite not a boy, on Boathouse Row,
Behind a waist-high fence of iron loops
That water lapped the ankles of,
I stood and watched in a dark light
Spilled out of an April sky ganged
With gaunt trailing black and gauzy clouds
The river roiling where land had been
The day before. I felt a terror then,
Not just for flesh, but for the first time
A fear that reached my fundamental self.

What I had known up till then as fixed,
What I had held firm as a banked-on
Certitude had suddenly come unloosed.
To see that solid width I had used
As a measuring line disappear
Caused in me and up-to-then unthought sense
Of the world's impermanence at base.

If the unbroken single direction,
Tamed and contained by civil works,
Which the river had always seemed
Could become this all-ways-at-once
Arching up in the middle muddiness—
Could prove in its passage able
To unsettle the seen and unseen earth together—
Upon what ground, no matter how high,
Could anyone surely, safely stand?

Former Altar Boy

That I have in my past put on black cassocks
And pulled stiff surplices over my eyes,
Lost briefly in the rustle of troubled starch,
Is as much a part of myself as the scars
That will mark my skin indelibly until my death.

More than a Lent and a half of years away in time
From the parish church where I knelt, bowed,
And rang a bell at the uplifted Host and Chalice,
I this night think again of the thick open *Missale,*
My having crossed with its heft to the Gospel side.

Because I served at Mass I still can say—
And will to the day my own tongue falls dead—
Some internalized immortal Latin words
That lie among my vocabulary's blunt Saxon ones
Like the flickering lights of a votive candle rack.

No longer innocent, I have all too many reasons
Now to recite a soft *Confiteor Deo...*
In any language I might know and move my fist
At each *mea culpa* to strike my breast—
My breast—but not the heart beneath that once beat there.

Requiescat

I think of him lying still as a Tenebrae deacon,
My never-to-be-old old friend dead of AIDS,
Stole crossing his heart hidden under a starched alb
And leaning on his breast a finger-tipped *Evangelium:*
That lover of watered-silk pom-pommed birettas,
Wide fiddleback chasubles woven of cloth-of-gold,
And sweet Palestrina sung by *contratenori.*

I met him, young, trapped together in a wrong age,
Arrived and flung late in time four centuries or so
Into an old Church reforming itself in anguish.
I watched him bewildered as altars turned around,
As the rhythm of the Latin Mass was abandoned

For an English prose so bad it hurt one's speaking mouth—
No wonder then the confusion that rose in his soul.

No less wonder the like confusion risen in his body:
With his skin of an olive tone and eyes as dark
And soft as any that were praised in Roman song.
He'd entered into the world as though designed
For a Tuscan noble's court of corrupt voluptuousness,
But was assigned by God's high irony only
To the puritan granite of Irish-American parish rectories.

I pray now he was met at the hour of his death by angels—
Some renegade border-crossing band of cherubim—
Who led him to such a place in Heaven as he would've wanted:
A small candle-bright chapel just off the main transept
Where quattrocento paintings, framed all in gold, hang
In which Our Lady and her Bambino smile and smile
Down on him amid the *putti*'s creased and folded baby fat.

On Learning of Nemerov's Death

I will this day, now that he no longer can,
Imagine his persona one more time
As he leaves the party in the living room
And goes to the kitchen where he settles
His glass, carefully emptied of spirits,
With a clink on the sink's ceramic counter,
Woofs a soft goodbye to the host's retriever,
And slips out the screen door, stopping its slap.

Now out under a night sky with no clouds,
He looks up to the stars he once flew among,
Still trying to measure the immense between,
Shakes his white-haired head at all the ignorance—
Including his own—to be found on earth,
Sights down the paved walk to the point at which
By perspective's law the lines all disappear,
And sets, sad navigator, a course for home.

Translating Brodsky

Under an order of banishment,
The poet walks with a measured tread
On airport tarmac dusted with snow,
Head down, hunched into his bulky coat,
Through the last vapors he will create,
Exhaling, out of his native air.
He carries to his non-scheduled flight
Only the little he could fit
In the bag kept packed for just this night.

Suddenly the plane gives off the sound
Of *coup de grace* shots as the pilot
Turns over first one slow turboprop,
Then the other, until, full throttle,
Two perfect crystal zeroes appear.
The poet climbs the steps of his craft
And vanishes with no backward glance,
Knowing—better than his deporters—
The etiquette of the exile's dance.

On a Line from "Song of Myself"

Surprised by an item in a Whitman roster
That had never registered before, though I'd read
The poem dozens of times, I watched words come
Leaping at me from the page: *The deacons
Are ordain'd with cross'd hands at the altar,*
And I suddenly imagined the half-crippled poet,
Ferried over from Camden, lurking in the rear
Of the old Basilica of Saints Peter and Paul,
Brownstoned and copper-roofed in Philadelphia—
But then I remembered, just scholar enough
To know that the *Song* was written early on,
During the simmering, simmering Brooklyn days,
And so any solemn liturgy of Holy Orders
He may have observed must have taken place
In some Manhattan pre-Saint Patrick's Cathedral.
Upstairs from where I am writing this is a book
On a shelf where lies the confirming date, but seeking
Truth, not fact, I will not yet rise up to check.

Rather, I will let Whitman stand where my heart
Wants him—in the deep gloom on the Epistle side
At the back of that hugely-envoulmed place, looking
Up to the lake of light spilled down from the dome
To where, robed in albs bleached and starched by nuns
To a white sharp enough to hurt the eye, young men lie
In silence face down on the sanctuary's marble floor
While over them an archbishop reads in Latin
From an oversized red leather-covered book, binding
The ordinands ever more deeply into a way of life
That Walt, watching the slender young males pledging
Their bodies away, could sense only as a waste,
As real to him as the physical waste he'd later see
Making his rounds in the aftermath military hospitals.
And I, who once feigned death on that cold shining floor,
Found myself with those truly dead deacons once again
In the great *Benedicite omnia opera* that is Whitman's poem
Linked as he said we all would be by his words across time,
Lurking now myself in the shadows of the Gospel side
Of my own unsanctuaried, stroke-hovering, wasted life.

Panta Rhei

March, 2003

They have borne helmets and body armor before,
These rivers, Tigris, Euphrates,
All the way back to those whose fear of The Afterlife
Was not of Hell, but Hades.

These waters have passed all manner of past empires
In history's ebb and flood
And will flow on indifferent to this latest influx,
This young American blood.

An American Memoir

With cancer in the mouth where command had been,
The old general sits cloaked in the weak winter's sun
Alone on a hotel's porch, empty in the heel of the year,
Reading the manuscript pages he'd written so far.
He goes over how as a boy he'd been most at ease
Not in the company of humans but among horses;
How his father had worn down a congressman
Into sending him to the grim grey school on the Hudson
Where, accepting a new name assembled in error,
He'd become an apprentice in the craft of war;
Of service in Mexico in a venture he knew to be immoral
Where the Virginian outranked him as a brevet colonel;
Of courtship, marriage, and then the separation forced
By his stationing at world's end, the California coast,
Where, lonely, he sank into a wet, hazy depression
That led to his half-demanded resignation;
And then six years of job after job with a lessening salary
Till there was nowhere but the stench of his father's tannery.

The last page written slides under, revealing the first.
Looking up the old man sees his breath's white mist
Like the ghostly smoke that lingers over a killing zone
And, least mystical of men, he notes no ominous sign,
Calculating only, like a quartermaster, the days left
By the cancer's slow investment of his body's fort.
The chapters remaining, he knows, will be easy to write,
So public did he become after rebellion broke out,
Able to consult all that the abstract archives hold,
The unfleshed accounts of what his blue battalions did.
Tired, he lets his cancer-ridden jaw lower and slip
Against his mufflered throat. He takes a soldier's nap
And dreams his one dream: it is of the incessant murder
That he ordered forth that first hour at Cold Harbor—
Six thousand needlessly dead. A sudden noise awakens him:
The gravel rattle of the rig come to take him home.
Riding in the black carriage, he resolves to express,
When it comes time to recount that hour, his only remorse.

Home Front

Amid TV flicker and toys left everywhere
By their preschool children, they wait, soldiers' wives,
Within the thin plasterboard walls of houses
On a base in the flat hot South Georgia sun
For the knock on the warped screen door
Of a chaplain with an officer in dress uniform,
Knowing their men now in a slow one-at-a-time war,
The huge assaults over, the carriers sailed home
To sunlit embraces on a San Diego pier.

Having heard white men in blue suits with red ties
Pronounce in Washington the objective achieved,
They wait in a deceptive American peace
Of Wal-Mart shopping, TV flicker, and toys,
Toys left everywhere by their preschool children,
Sure that any one of them might be handed soon—
Under murmured words of a nation's gratitude
From the mouth of a gold-braided Honor Guardsman—
The soft three-cornered pillow of a folded flag.

Skandalon

I think of my seminary classmates,
Surely some of them portly pastors by now,
Smoking long cigars and driving big sedans.

I imagine each waving to the schoolboys
On the streets of his parish as he glides by
As Father Lambert often waved to me

From his black and chrome Oldsmobile 98,
Happy to have been so singled out by
One of my small town's most eminent men.

It saddens me to think how such boys today—
Taught well by their wary, anxious mothers—
Have to look back with narrowed eyes, wondering.

The Junk Farm

Beside a barn so nearly down it seemed
Itself merely a heap of boards, he had heaped
Haphazard piles of worn-out things he'd dragged
Homeward from miles around for years and years,
Sensing somehow in each some someday use.

What filled finally that hillside farm's field
Gave off in its separateness no surprise:
The ordinary ruck of the broken-
Apart parts of all man-assembled things—
Tires without tread, bedsprings, old mowers,
Oil cans, car fenders, and barbed, rusting wires
Feigning here and there the natural look
Of the tree-trapping vines that winter shows forth

Yet more than once in the low sun's last light,
Driving by—unconsciously speeding up
As I neared, passed, and raced downroad away—
If the old white-haired, mackinawed man
Was shifting among it all, it all shaped
Together around him—its mind—and grew,
Out of confusion, something single—something new.

Northbound

Into what darkness have they all gone by now,
Those passengers on the trains that sixty years ago
Passed over my head while I rowed beneath
The bridge that bore them over the Schuylkill's flow?

Young and ignorant I gave them never a thought,
Minding only the motion of my moving oar,
Never even hearing above me what I know in age
Must have been in fact a deafening roar.

Old now, I rise from reverie and ride with them
Stone arch by stone arch into the coming night,
And do not look down on my fragile boat below
Spidering upstream in the late day's light.

The City Game

No greensward English playing fields,
These chainlinked plains of asphalt
With netless rings raised more or less
Ten feet up a pole or fixed on a wall
Where, swaggering like Seventeenth
Century foppish Cavaliers,
Young angry blacks observe still
The conventions of *braggadocio,*
Backed always with whatever steel-
Quick movements of muscles might be
Required. Seeing them in small edge-
Of-battle clumps hurling their bodies
Into the mass, attempting to rise
Above it all, inside the strict conventions
By which they referee themselves,
My over-educated suburban baseball eyes
Turn them, as I drive safely by,
Into so many improvising early poets,
Stylizing with rhythm, inventing ways
To introduce new forms into an old, old court.

The Passing of the Radio Generation

Who knows what evil lurks...
        radio theme phrase, 1936-1956

Saturdays, through many double-featured hours,
They watched a wall of light where Tarzan swung
And Gene Autry sang and Buck Rogers
Soared about space in a blacked-out soundstage.
Come war, they hissed the Nazis in the newsreels.

On Wednesdays *Colliers*, the *Post, Look,* and *Life*
Arrived with cartoons, photos, and fiction in the mail,
Shaping their knowledge of a more innocent world—

But every evening of the week, they listened
To what came out of thin air through the static-filled
Paper-covered speakers straight into their ears
And minds, making for themselves memories
They have fewer and fewer others to share with now.

Televisions flutter unseen, scarcely heard, in other rooms
As they wait in their kitchens for tea water to boil
In the shadow of what The Shadow was said to know.

Old, Old Story

Sidewise, she had kept her eye on its growing,
That apple sagging down near her face.
She knew it held the way to further knowing,
But fear stayed her hand. She left it in its place—

Till that morning she learned to her surprise
That she could understand a serpent's speech.
Swaying, she looked into black, staring eyes
And heard a sibilant command to reach.

The rest you know. At least, you ought to know.
And did it really happen? Eve and Tree
And Snake and Adam? Something did. That's so.
Just take a look around the world. You'll see—

Hands are grasping yet and the snake is coiled
To teach us still: desire gained, desire spoiled.

A Vision of Heaven in, Oh, Let's Say, Soperton, GA

Though no eyes but my own weakening ones
May ever admit these words into a mind
Other than my own weakening one, still
Will I write, wondering where something
Either in or out of this world will lead me—
And now, I do not know how, the words
Become a freight train, slowly bisecting
A small mid-Georgia town with a jumble
Of different heavily-laden cars all designed
To carry various kinds of bespoke cargoes—
Kaolin, bituminous coal, chemicals,
And pine logs uniformly cut for pulpwood—
All of it united only in its simply being
Hauled as a congregate at this moment
Down parallel lines that behave as Euclid
Discovered they must and never, ever meet
While at each crossing rutted asphalt road
Behind lowered striped flimsy wooden gates
People sit in turned-off rusted pickup trucks
Or in old GM sedans with ticking cylinders
And wait angrily for their free passage over,
And only children and other childlike ones
Who are still in the habit of keeping count
Not only do not grumble but in fact rejoice
For having been stayed so involuntarily
And stunned into patient bewilderment
As a sudden unity makes itself manifest
In the middle of this multifold contrivance
That is perhaps not our only universe.

Casuistical

In my rented-from-Alamo Buick,
Stopped for a red light in the right hand lane
Westbound on Route 30 in Lancaster,
I looked up and to my left and, surprised, saw
In the passenger seat of a new Dodge pickup
A Plain Person, black suit, straw hat, beard and all.

I was puzzled, having passed horse-drawn buggies
All that morning and seen for the first time in years
Clothes pegged out to dry on backyard lines.
Later that day I learned that *The Ordnung*
Permitted the hiring of a non-Amish
To drive one about on business errands.

I thought then of the Orthodox Jews,
Each family employing a *Shabbes goy*
To perform forbidden necessary tasks,
Such as the lighting of fires for cooking
Or, more recently, flipping a switch
To bring more light than any menorah's.

Ready to think hypocrisy, I remembered
Suddenly how in my own Catholic boyhood
We awaited the Cardinal-Archbishop's
Permission, through pastors in local pulpits,
Allowing us to eat leftover turkey
On the Friday after every Thanksgiving Day.

Oh, keeping the Law of the Lord is hard
In Latin, Hebrew, or Pennsylvania Dutch.
One needs all the help one can get to cross
The narrow passages, the minefield miles,
Yet, I'm sure, like any father with small children.
Our *Abba* looks down, nods his head, and smiles.

Addicted

I open a box marked Winston
And extract a tube of death—
Another one for shortening
My allotted store of breath.

It was an Englishman named Raleigh
Who brought tobacco back
And taught all the world the way
Of dying pack by pack.

I keep persisting like a fool,
Drawing smoke across my tongue,
Ignoring what is happening--
The blackening of each lung.

I know one day that I will quit
This habit and this sin:
The day my body's finally done
With pulling air within.

Exile

Old now and never to return
He totals up a memory's tally.
Tracing a blue-lined boyhood creek
On a page of Rand McNally.

Far off the remembered waters
Seek a dark river, a darker sea
He sets the atlas on a shelf
Knowing that somehow so does he.

Testament

A row of book spines on a flea market table
Provoked the inference that a man had died.
Only death releases such volumes as these—
By titles alone an entire life implied.

European art books, lives of composers,
A Hungarian lexicon—the native tongue?
I imagined him a Fifties refugee
Fleeing for Western freedom when he was young.

Choosing two books, I paid three dollars
And walked away with something new in mind:
Knowing my own death to be never far off,
I thought of the telltale books I'll leave behind.

Change

Overwhelmed by the cellular tsunami,
Even the open wall-mounted pay phones
Are headed for the black oblivion
Of those boxes with a collapsing door
Into which Clark Kent dashed many years before.

In this new world, where now will children find
Smooth cool coin slots to put their fingers in,
Always with a hesitant tremor of hope
That maybe, just maybe, *this* magic time
They'll touch the silver of an unclaimed dime?

Memory

If God come to me, He must by His own design
Come to me along Rigby, Baltimore, Wycombe,
Stewart, Stratford, Highland, and all the other
Avenues of my Quaker-founded boyhood town.
Oh, God, I do not—searcher for a single truth—
Envy You the multiple paths to the human heart
You must follow, seeking us in the streets of our youth.

At the intersection of Lansdowne and Garrett,
Every quarter hour there was imposed on traffic
The passing of the Red Arrow Line's slow trolleys.
How comes it, God—all these later years along
I find myself in a daydream—oh God , it is so strange—
Idling in a car at that place of crossing roads,
Waiting for the gates to lift, for the light to change?

December: April Flood

In the dead of a southern winter, old,
How is it that I can be young again,
Be leaning over the chest-high-to-a-boy
Pebbled concrete upstream wall of a bridge
That bears Scottdale Road over Darby Creek,
And with fear again see rushing down at me
After three thunderstorming April days
Roiled olive waters streaked with red and brown
Filling nearly the arch I stand above?

I watch with fascinated mind the things
I know all at once are what the word *wrack*
With its *double-u* exactly describes:
Leafy tree branches, ripsawed free by lightning,
Black sodden planks from a broken-apart shed,
Amber beer bottles dislodged from bushes
In which they'd landed a month earlier
Flung from the open windows of cars
That had been sealed through all the winter.

In order to make the madness flow away
I cross the asphalt to the far railing, look down,
And spy one sponge rubber ball, lost—I guess—
On a small town's street by a child sobbing
To see it roll from his life toward the grin
Of a black satanic storm sewer's mouth
To be swept to the end of its bouncing life,
Bobbing in the smooth back-swirling eddy
Formed behind the bridge's bulky central pier.

I lift up my thoughts from the swollen stream
And pass all the bridges standing beyond me
Till I make in my mind that marshy place
Where the creek keeps on darkly disappearing
Into the slow Delaware's wider waters,
Destined themselves for loss elsewhere at sea,
And I know, old in this southern winter,
What I had not, young, in that northern spring:
We are all wrack—tumbled—in a higher flood.

From the Craft

I lower lines with thin curved hooks
Worm-hidden into dark waters.
Though wounded, the worms writhe free.
Bare, my barbs dangle still down there,
Ignored by the swift schooling fish
Who have just sucked wide-openmouthed
Some bait without a death inside.
Nor do all my nets not unknot.

Cargo

Hauled by a harnessed beast, no clipper, no yacht,
But a broad-beamed canal barge, safely embraced by banks
And hawsered fast aside at the storm's first black threat,
I am making the slow voyage, leaving behind a weak wake,
So low and barely white as to be almost invisible, lock-
Lifted, lock lowered, by the civilly engineered past,
When the dragging gravity of the world makes its oppose—
Inwardly proud, though, to be bearing for the Master of Loads
Much that will rise in the end on roped slings from my dark hold.

A NOTE OF THANKS-GIVING

This book of retrospection affords me the opportunity to express gratitude to at least a few fellow workers in the craft of poetry. They are in my mind clustered as a constellation in my personal night sky. That constellation's name is Callanwolde, the arts center in Atlanta that has for nearly fifty years now been a place where every month people who care about the art gather to hear poems and meet as a community. Thanks to Callanwolde I have had the grace of being encouraged to keep alive a care for verse in all its manifestations.

First, the elegiac. Thanks to Callanwolde I have known great souls whom I miss and who are called to mind every time I go through its doors: Turner Cassity, John Stone, Joseph Young, Ron Hendricks, and Chuck Robertson.

Among the living first of all has to be Eugene Ellis* who was the architect of Callanwolde's continued success, bringing to Atlanta's some of the best poets of his time, poets of the stature of Howard Nemerov, Anthony Hecht, Richard Hugo, Adrienne Rich, as well as giving a hearing to fine Georgia poets like Alicia Stallings, Walter Griffin, Memye Curtis Tucker, M. Ayodele Heath and Rosemary Daniell to name only a few of the hundreds and hundreds of readers who count their time at Callanwolde as a high point in their poetic lives.

I must thank, too, the current members of the Poetry Committee at Callanwolde: Ruth and Stephen Windham whose energy and enthusiasm make the readings a successful enterprise, and Dan Veach whose service to poetry, both locally and internationally, has been heroic.

Poetry has to be one of the loneliest arts, but those named above and so many others I have not mentioned (because of a faulty memory) have made mine less lonely.

* While this book was in production Gene died; I lost one of my best friends and my most perceptive reader.

INDEX OF TITLES

Note: The clerihews and double dactyls in this book do not have titles. In this index of titles the clerihews are listed by their first line followed by the word "clerihew" in parentheses; and the double dactyls, which all begin with the first line "Higgledy-piggledy," are listed by their second line followed by the words "double dactyl" in parentheses.

Following this index are an index of clerihew subjects and an index of double dactyl subjects, both with the subjects listed alphabetically by last name.

INDEX OF DOUBLE DACTYL SUBJECTS

INDEX OF CLERIHEW SUBJECTS